MY FRIEND FIGARO
(LESSONS FROM A FLY)

A book on change management for personal and organizational growth and adaptability.

IKENNA ANYADIKE

MY FRIEND FIGARO

(Lessons From a Fly)

A book on change management for personal and organizational growth and adpatability.

IKENNA ANYADIKE

◆ ◆ ◆

COPYRIGHT (C) 2021 BY IKENNA ANYADIKE.

All rights reserved. No part of this book may be reproduced, stored in a retrieval system or transmitted in any form or by any means, electronic, mechanical, photocopying, recording or otherwise, without the prior written permission of the author.

Requests to the author for permission should be addressed to:

Ikenna Anyadike | anyadike.ikenna@gmail.com

Abuja, Nigeria.

CAVEAT

◆ ◆ ◆

The following is a work of fiction and isn't targeted at any individual. All seeming allusions to real life characters are coincidental. No copy of this work should be reproduced, reposted or circulated in any form without the express permission of the copyright owner.

"MY FRIEND FIGARO" is a single story partitioned into episodes for maximum understanding. Please follow the sequence of the story all the way to the end. Take some time to reflect on the principles highlighted in the book and feel free to share the story and the seven principles with your circle(s) of influence.

If you would like to get in touch with the author, please call or write: anyadike.ikenna@gmail.com | +234-803-867-3143

CONTENT

Episode 1: How it all began.
Episode 2: Dead? Yes Dead!
Episode 3: Reminiscence.
Episode 4: There.
Episode 5: Voila!
Episode 6: Ready... Set... Buzz!
Episode 7: The Chase.
Episode 8: The Escape.
Episode 9: Harmed.
Episode 10: Switch Tactics? No!
Episode 11: Squished.
Episode 12: My Burden.
Episode 13: Given.
Episode 14: Influenced? No.
Episode 15: Fast... Furious.
Episode 16: Ride Out.
Episode 17: Peril? Maybe.
Episode 18: Control.
Episode 19: Drive.
Episode 20: Denouement.

EPISODE 1.

HOW IT ALL BEGAN…

Figaro was my friend, yes my friend; he was a fly who loved to live his life to the best of all that life offered. He was a fly with a wonderful personality, awesome sense of humor, well-known in our neighborhood for his witty remarks and easy approach to life. He never took himself too seriously and he always had a witty remark for everything and everyone. If Figaro wanted to tell you not to disturb him, he would rather say, "Buzz off" (*laughs*). In all, he was a great fly.

His girlfriend adored him because he was also a great provider, he had an acute sense of smell and he could sniff out food even from unimaginable distances and then embark on a systematic search till he found it. He was smart too as he could take in information faster than most flies I know. However, Figaro had one maxim and that was his undoing, it was **"keep at it till it budges"**. He was quite stubborn in keeping up with this principle.

EPISODE 2.

DEAD? YES DEAD.

I'm sure by now you must be wondering why I keep referring to my friend Figaro in the past tense? Well, that is because Figaro is dead, as in D-E-A-D.

He can't do any flying, can't sniff out food anymore, can't give any witty or smart catchy lines as was his custom, can't do anything anymore.

What happened to Figaro? Well Figaro died on account of his stubbornness and refusal to adapt to change.

I remember spending time with Figaro when he was alive, talking about strategies, flight modes and skills on how to avert danger. You know that a fly's life is riddled with danger. From humans, insecticides, suffocation and all sorts, but then, that's what makes the life of a fly exciting. The ability to evade all barriers set up by humans and yet survive with the "prize", that's the pride of being a fly. I wouldn't have wished to be any other insect (*winks*).

EPISODE 3.

REMINISCENSE...

How did Figaro die? Well here's the story.

It was a bright and sunny day and I was lounging in a heap of compost in Flyville tending to my business when Figaro excitedly landed and told me that his "nasal compass" (*one of his witty remarks*) had picked up a pleasant aroma and he would like us to go check the place out, dig in and get gone. He said it was a sting operation, no risks.

Honestly, I had some misgivings about the idea, primarily because I wasn't really hungry as I was already tending to "business" on the heap of compost. But the idea sounded really alluring and Figaro wasn't going to take "No" for an answer, even if I had declined he still would have gone ahead with the adventure.

So I figured there was nothing to lose by tagging along with him, I still had my heap of compost waiting for me, it was mine and it wasn't going anywhere without my permission. Again it isn't everyday that we flies get to dig into some really nice and fresh-from-the-pot human food.

I saddled up and both of us buzzed off.

Figaro's excitement was quite contagious, he kept doing acrobatic flips, taking dives and thrusts that I wouldn't imagine doing myself. His excitement was written all over him, Figaro had hit it big.

IKENNA ANYADIKE

What we didn't know was what life had in store for us on that ill-fated mission.

EPISODE 4.

THERE...

When we arrived at our destination which was a really massive house in a really nice neighbourhood, the first thing I noticed was that there weren't a lot of flies around, and the few that buzzed past us all kept to their businesses, none as much as looked in our direction. My self-preservation instincts kicked in and I became cautious.

The lessons I learnt in Flyville Aviation Academy came flooding back to me. We were taught as newbie fliers learning to fly that the first thing to do on a mission such as the one we were currently embarked upon was to do a **"reconnoiter flight sequence"** on our target before homing in for the "kill" (*my expression for digging-in/landing*).

As longtime fliers Figaro and I did all the required preliminary reconnaissance to ensure that the coast was actually clear. The major essence of the reconnoiter flight sequence is to discover other secondary escape routes to facilitate easy escape in the event of possible sealing off and closure of the primary entry point by possible hostiles.

Figaro always prided in the fact that he had never used a secondary escape route to facilitate his escape, as he had always outwitted hostile assailants by escaping through the primary point of entry. To him, it was one way in and the same way out. He was Figaro the fly. All the flies at Flyville marveled at this record-breaking feat of Figaro's.

Rumour had it one time that Figaro was cornered by hostiles waving brooms, fly-swatters and horse-tail fly catchers but he outwitted the hostiles and escaped without as much as a scratch. Indeed Figaro had perfected the art of escape.

What made Figaro a super-fly and larger than life was that he never ever took the pains of scouting for a secondary escape point; he was too "fly" for that, he was Figaro the Fly!

EPISODE 5.

VOILA...!

We found our entry point in no time at all, got into the house, made our way as cautiously as we could through the massive hall where the human occupants called family - *I think that is what humans call the gathering of the elder male, elder female and young hatchlings of their species* - were all gathered.

We made our way all the way to the primary target zone from where the aroma came. By the time we got there, all my fly instincts and guards were let down and replaced with such a craving for the source of the alluring aroma.

I glanced sideways at Figaro and noticed the sublime joy written all over his face. I smiled to myself as we headed to the main source of the aroma guided by our fly-sense and multi-dimensional compound eyes. The source was a steaming pan of freshly made pie with such an aroma that could make any fly go "buzzy" - *a term that describes when a fly goes "crazy", as humans put it.*

Here we were, staring at this freshly made pan of pie, hot and sizzling, spiced up and ready to go. My proboscis mechanism immediately initiated automatically having been primed, serviced and 'oiled' earlier for maximum efficiency.

EPISODE 6.

READY... SET... BUZZ!

Figaro and I went in for the "kill", landed on the pie and took our respective positions. We engaged our proboscis, lumped it with mucous for easy conversion to fluid and then went to work, taking in as much as we could.

We hadn't been there long before we suddenly heard a piercing shriek. When I heard it, I directed my multidimensional compound eyes towards the shriek, while at the same time lifting into the air because that was the safest place to be at that material time given the circumstance.

What I saw frightened me to my bones.

The entire family of hostiles had all sorts of injurious equipments, and they were coming towards us. I was already airborne, but my friend Figaro having relaxed his guard a little too much wasn't as quick to lift off the food as I was.

EPISODE 7.

THE CHASE.

His fatal mistake was his erroneous assumption that he had everything covered; this cocky assumption had finally put him in the 'spot'.

I immediately made my way toward the primary entry point only to discover that the hostiles had sealed it off. Instinctively, I made for the secondary escape route which I had earlier discovered upon our arrival during the reconnoiter flight sequence. My adrenalin level was at an all time high as I made for my only means of escape from the horrible trap we had 'walked' into.

I heard Figaro call out to me, but my fly-senses had already initiated the self-preservation mode, and I wasn't going to get caught neither was I going to die out there on an adventure I had embarked upon against my sense of better judgment. I remembered my heap of compost yet unfinished and regretted tagging along with Figaro on this deadly adventure.

EPISODE 8.

THE ESCAPE.

I got to the secondary escape point in record time. A record that surprised me greatly nonetheless. I squeezed myself through the tiny crack large enough for only one fly at a time as the heavy thud of my assailant's fly-swatter missed me by a hair's breath.

At last I was free of the danger, outside in the open, and away from the mean hostiles in the awful house. Suddenly, I remembered that Figaro was still inside the house with the entire mob of hostiles who were determined not to let him escape.

I flew close to the big transparent wall - *I think humans call it window* -, took a look and what I saw sent chills down my spine (*not that I have a spine anyway, I'm just talking*).

Figaro had the entire company of hostiles close at his heels, determined to splatter him to pieces. He knew his assailants were not in any way letting him off without at least hurting him. And this situation wasn't like any other he had previously been in. It was "fly or die" for Figaro, and he perfectly understood that.

He did all the flight manoeuvres he knew. Pulled all the stunts he could all in his attempt to shake off the hostiles, but they weren't letting him out of their sight.

EPISODE 9.

HARMED...

Their indignation I think was borne out of the fact that by reason of our activity on the pie, it had become inedible and virtually harmful for human consumption.

The truth is, they were actually right, because whatever we flies perch on, especially food, it instantly becomes infested with germs that cause quite a number of diseases to humans. I feel I owe it to Figaro to come clean with the truth as he would have wanted me to.

That being said, I don't feel any form of remorse about this. I mean, we flies have to eat as well for the ecosystem to be maintained, but that is by the way.

(Let's get back to the story)...

While I perched outside watching the unfolding drama inside the house with horror, I knew Figaro was in for it this time. Frankly, I didn't see any way he could have escaped. The odds were heavily stacked against him.

EPISODE 10.

SWITCH TACTICS? NO.

Something struck me however. I noticed that Figaro's efforts at escape was concentrated on looking for a way to fly out through our primary point of entrance, the point I told you earlier was blocked off by the hostiles.

Honestly I couldn't understand what he was thinking in that moment. I frantically signalled for him to head towards the secondary escape point through which I myself had earlier escaped by a hair's breathe.

Alas, Figaro wasn't one to listen to advice. He persistently kept pushing against the entry point that wouldn't budge. He kept throwing himself at it, hitting against it with no results.

I tried getting his attention again to signal to him that what he was doing was an exercise in futility. The only escape route available to him was the alternative one which he needed to get to if he wanted to survive the horror he was in.

I guess Figaro felt he had it all under control even in the heat of that danger. He was determined to break through the entry point that wouldn't budge, completely neglecting the secondary escape point which was unguarded and would have let him out safely.

EPISODE 11.

SQUISHED!

At last, while he was still struggling to break through the familiar point through which we got into the house, his strength failed him and his assailants came heavily upon him with all the weapons they had.

I couldn't bear to watch anymore. I couldn't bear to see my friend Figaro turned into a mash of fly-mess.

Till date, I have not been able to erase the look of intense horror on Figaro's face when he knew his end had come, shortly before that deadly fly-swatter smashed the life out of him against the transparent wall.

I see Figaro's last look in my sleep, when eating and when at work. That was the look of horror on the face of a fly who felt he had it all under control, and refused to adapt and change strategy when the occasion clearly demanded it.

EPISODE 12.

MY BURDEN.

I have therefore taken it as my personal burden to share the story of the death of my friend Figaro and the lessons I have since learnt from it.

Figaro my friend spurned change, and he "got served" for it.

A human by name Heraclitus once said, **"Change is the fundamental nature of reality"**, and I'll add mine that goes thus, **"when you spurn change, you may not live to tell the story"**. We flies know and hold this principle to be true.

Figaro figured this out eventually at death.

Another human named Charles Darwin also made a profound statement in line with change which I love so much. He said **"It is not the strongest of the species that survives or the most intelligent, but the ones most responsive to change"**.

That said, I can tell you from a fly's standpoint that change is about survival.

Figaro thought he knew this, but he didn't quite get the full import of the survival part.

EPISODE 13.

GIVEN. With respect to the memory of my friend Figaro, I feel mandated to share seven principles about change having had time to reflect deeply on the subject of understanding and mastering change.

Here I go:

Change is a given.

Nothing ever remains rigid and immobile in this life. I can tell you that categorically having lived as a fly for some time now. That is why we have night and day, sun and rain. Isn't it obvious?

I have even heard humans say that the earth rotates and spins round and round. I haven't been able to wrap my fly-brain around that fact yet. It is not as though I doubt it. I just have my some reservations about it. I may be wrong anyway.

In any case, the fact of the matter is that change is a given. It is bound to happen and it always happens.

EPISODE 14.

INFLUENCED? NO.

Change must happen irrespective of our conscious application of any form of influence.

It is best to anticipate change so that when it eventually happens we wouldn't be caught off-guard having made secondary routes/channels of escape to cushion the effect it would have on us when it finally comes.

I have since learnt that it is better to prepare for change and it ends up not coming, than being unprepared and have it blindside you.

My mantra is, "STAY READY ... BE PREPARED".

EPISODE 15.

FAST...FURIOUS.

Change is fast.

I couldn't agree more with this principle. I still remember how quickly the situation changed on the day that Figaro met his demise.

One moment we were enjoying the steaming pan of pie, oblivious to any danger, the next moment we were flying to save our lives.

When change happens, it usually does so with speed. You have to match it pace for pace if you are to survive.

EPISODE 16.

RIDE OUT.

Change will take you for a ride if you are not aware of it.

It is infinitely good sense to seek out alternative avenues that will lead you to escape in the event of a sudden change.

I can't imagine what would have happened to me if I hadn't scouted around for a secondary escape route on that fateful day.

Maybe, I would have been like Figaro ...(*shudders*).

EPISODE 17.

Peril? Maybe.

Change is not apologetic.

When change happens, it usually doesn't come pleading and negotiating with you. As a matter of fact, it usually seems to blindside you, especially if you have not prepared adequately before time.

I still remember the sudden appearance of our hostile assailants with any prior notification. Figaro and I were boxed in before we realized what had happened to us. Our primary escape point, which was our entry point was sealed off before we could get there.

I advise you to imbibe this principle and you will never be surprised. I heard a human named Sun Tzu, a renowned war strategist make the following statement, "**Know your enemy, know yourself and in a hundred battles you will never be in peril**".

Your enemy here is change, know him and know yourself so that when it battles against you, you will never be in peril.

EPISODE 18.

CONTROL.

Change can be controlled.

I know you may have heard it said that certain things are in the realm of happenstance, and that very little can be controlled.

My intention is to help you understand and internalize all of the principles I have mentioned. By so doing, you will be well on your way to mastering change as you will be positioned with all the advantages and the knowledge needed to control change as it comes your way.

EPISODE 19.

RIVE.

Drive the change.

This last principle is more or less an instruction that you are required to comply with if you desire to live long in this dangerous and perilous world as a fly.

The responsibility of understanding, anticipating and learning the rudiments of change together with the skills needed to drive it are entirely up to you.

I sincerely hope you don't dissappoint me.

EPISODE 20.

DENOUMENT.

I just realized that all of these principles were all latent in my subconscious before I condensed them for you.

I would like you adhere to these principles as failure to do so will set you on the same path as my friend Figaro. They can literally determine whether you live or die.

I guess I'll stop right here. I have a heap of decaying compost to "attend" to. I am sure you know that a fly has got to do what a fly has to do. (*Winks*)

MARTIN THE FLY.

◆ ◆ ◆

THE END.

ABOUT THE AUTHOR

Ikenna Anyadike is an entrepreneur and personality development coach who is passionate about people development.

He is in charge of running the day to day activities of CONNOISSEEUR CONSULTS, a training and consulting outfit with a portfolio that stretches from corporate boardrooms to school classrooms and from corporate blue-bloods to teenage students in his quest to catalyze the needed self-awareness individuals require to trigger their next level.

He is an expert in teen/youth development specifically in the area of catalyzing the mental and intellectual shift needed by young people to effectively handle the demands of the now and the future.

Through his several projects, he has significantly molded and still continues to mold the intellectual capital of young people(students) through the unique programs on those platforms.

He has written several articles in newspapers and magazines.

"My Friend Figaro" is his first published work.

www.ingramcontent.com/pod-product-compliance
Lightning Source LLC
Chambersburg PA
CBHW030046230526
45472CB00005B/1695